JAZZ GUITAR SOLOING

By Bob Patterson

A How-To-Guide To The Scales, Arpeggios And Licks Needed In Improvising Jazz On The Guitar In An Easy To Follow Format

Catalog No. B72
ISBN 0-7935-5101-3

7777 W. BLUEMOUND RD. P.O. BOX 13819 MILWAUKEE, WI 53213

© 1995 Houston Publishing, Inc.
224 South Lebanon Street, Lebanon, IN, 46052, USA
All Rights Reserved   International Copyright Secured   Printed in the USA

TABLE OF CONTENTS

INTRODUCTION 1

HAND POSITIONS 2

SCALES 3

A SHORT BREATHER 9

MODES 11

DIMINISHED SCALES 17

WHOLETONE SCALES 21

MODES II 24

PENTATONICS AND THE BLUES 28

LICKS 33

TURNAROUNDS 42

CHEAP TRICKS 43

PLAYING OVER CHANGES 45

PROGRESSION ANALYSIS 53

CHORD/SCALE USAGE CHART 56

INTRODUCTION

Over the years of learning and playing jazz on the guitar, coupled with sitting through many lessons (both as student and teacher), I have started to notice that certain concepts have been consistently valid. No matter what approach a teacher or player might take, there are a number of methods that continually seem to hold true. In this book, I have tried to put many of these methods together in an easy-to-digest format that will aid the beginning or intermediate jazz guitarist in their quest for improvement. Any true student wants to be better no matter how good he or she is at the moment; so I hope this book will be of special value to those with that desire to improve.

I have intended this book for people who can already play the guitar a little; who know something about chords and lead playing, but want to be able to play jazz solos. I would suggest picking up a good chord encyclopedia if some of the chords mentioned here seem foreign. I don't want to waste time explaining information that is much more thoroughly covered in someone else's book!

The guitar is an especially difficult instrument to master. It's not as physically demanding as the piano or trumpet, but the juxtapositioning of 6 strings with 20-24 frets contains many little complexities that make it difficult for the player to execute ideas at will (which is the ultimate goal of the improvisor). Therefore, we have to learn how to deal with the FINGERING and POSITIONING of notes before dealing with the notes themselves musically.

Because of that, I believe that learning to play jazz solos on the guitar must first involve raw technical mastery. After all, you have to learn to spell before you can write a story, don't you? Once a level of technical proficiency is achieved and honed to the point of instinct (where you don't have to consciously THINK about what you are doing, but just do it), the player can then deal with more musical and creative aspects of jazz improvisation.

I will be especially picky about the technical aspects of playing at first, simply because I believe in the value of repetition. That is the only way to achieve "muscle memory." Later on, I will ignore (or even break) the rules I harp on initially. That's because by that time they should've automatically crept into your playing if you've followed the lessons as outlined. Don't get frustrated! Be patient at first; it will pay off in the long run.

Some of the examples are given both in normal notation and tablature. There are also fingering diagrams here and there. I am a firm believer in the importance of sight reading, but I understand how hard it is for most guitarists! I'll take it easy on you for now, but practice your reading. You'll thank me later.

This book is not exhaustive. There may be some things you know that I haven't included here. That's okay. Don't forget that this book is for jazz beginners, with enough information to provide a good grounding in the art of improvisation. Once you have a mastery of the "building blocks," you will be well on your way to finding your own voice as a jazz guitar soloist.

HOW TO PRACTICE

Your practice time will be much better spent if you follow a few simple guidelines. You'll be surprised at the rapid progress you can make if you stick to them.

1) Choose a practice area free of distractions. Turn off the TV, disconnect the phone if you can (thank God for answering machines!), and make sure you have sufficient light.

2) Get a straight-back chair with no arms, a music stand, and a metronome (there are many inexpensive electronic models out now - this is VERY important).

3) Choose a type of guitar pick you like and STICK with it. The thickness of the pick has a big effect on your

playing. The same goes for string gauges and guitar strap lengths. You should adjust your strap so that it holds the guitar in roughly the same position standing as sitting. You may not look as cool as your favorite heavy metal hero, but you'll play better.

4) Don't feel guilty if you lack the endurance to practice for hours on end. It's not always good for you anyway. You can make a lot of progress on 45 minutes to 1 hour a day. But, you must CONSISTENTLY practice daily.

HAND POSITIONS

Before you begin the exercises in this book, I should say a few words about correct hand positioning. Your left hand (LH) should not "palm" the neck of the guitar. In fact, it should not touch the neck at all except for the thumb and fingertips. Keep the thumb flat on the back of the neck (roughly opposite the 2nd finger), resisting the tendency to wrap it over the top. As for your right hand (RH), don't anchor the wrist on the guitar. Keep the wrist up and free, contacting the guitar body only at a point just below the elbow. Hold the pick securely and keep your RH wrist slightly bent down. This may feel unnatural at first, but it will soon afford you much flexibility and speed down the road.

FINGERING EXERCISE

This will serve as an excellent drill for finger independence, hand coordination, picking technique, etc. It may seem monotonous and even tedious at first, but stick with it. This exercise provides long-term benefits.

1) Set your metronome to approximately 80 beats per minute.

2) Starting at the 6th string 1st fret, play the following pattern (in quarter notes):

```
|  1  |  2  |  3  |  4  |
|  1  |  2  |  3  |  4  |
|  1  |  2  |  3  |  4  |
|  1  |  2  |  3  |  4  |
|  1  |  2  |  3  |  4  |
|  1  |  2  |  3  |  4  |
```

3) Without dropping a beat, shift your hand up 1 fret, then play the same pattern REVERSED (that is, 4-3-2-1 back down to the 6th string 2nd fret).

4) Move up one fret and repeat step 2 in the new position.

The idea is to play 1-2-3-4 up the strings and 4-3-2-1 back down. Continue this process all the way up the fretboard, then back. This should take about 5 1/2 minutes. If you make any mistakes, slow down the tempo. Go as slow as necessary to get it perfect! As you feel more comfortable, you can increase the tempo. Remember: **speed should come naturally.**

While playing this exercise you should try to get an even, full tone from all the notes. Remember what I said about hand positions and apply those rules here. This is also a good drill for alternate picking. Keep strict up/down picking going at all times. Try to get the same tone from your upstrokes that you get from your downstrokes. Avoid "flams" (hitting the string with your finger an instant before you pick the note).

When you're playing the 1-2-3-4 part of this drill, don't lift your LH fingers off the strings. Keep them where they are and resist the urge to move your left hand.

There are quite a few variations to this drill that you should also try. The fingering combinations become much more difficult but help to develop flexibility and independence in all 4 LH fingers, as well as some independence between the hands. Here they are:

UP	DOWN
1234	4321
1243	3421
1324	4231
1342	2431
1423	3241
1432	2341
2134	4312
2143	3412
2314	4132
2341	1432
2413	3142
2431	1342
3124	4213
3142	2413
3214	4123
3241	1423
3412	2143
3421	1243
4123	3214
4132	2314
4213	3124
4231	1324
4312	2134
4321	1234

Try at least 2 or 3 of these a day to start off your practice session. They are excellent warmups. I guarantee you, if these drills don't drive you crazy first, you will end up with a great deal of hand flexibility. You will also have played every theoretical combination of fingers on any given string, and become used to leading to the next string (up or down) with any finger. They are also good for getting warmed up quickly when you don't have time to run through your scales!

SCALES

Knowledge of scales is absolutely essential to improvising jazz. And by knowledge, I don't mean just being able to play the scale up and down. You should be able to play them in 3rds, 4ths, 6ths, etc. Basically, you should know them inside out. There are as many ways to practice them as you can think of. I will show a few ways that have helped me.

For the most part, the patterns will be two octaves long, starting and ending on the root. In many cases you can extend the fingerings beyond what I have given, but I have laid them out so as to reinforce the sound of the root in your ear. You will also notice that the root of the scale is always highlighted.

MAJOR SCALES

Major scales are probably the most important scale types you will ever need as a jazz improvisor. You can use the major scale over any Major, Maj 7, Maj 6, 6/9, or Maj add 9 chord, primarily when it is the tonic (ex: Fmaj7 in the key of F). Here is the C major scale:

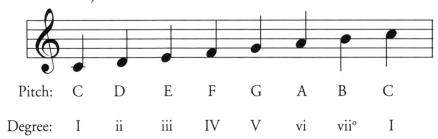

Pitch:	C	D	E	F	G	A	B	C
Degree:	I	ii	iii	IV	V	vi	vii°	I

From the major scale patterns, you can derive all three types of minor scales (natural, harmonic, melodic) and all modes, with their related arpeggios. For that reason, you should endeavor to totally digest this section of the book. These fingerings need to become as natural to you as breathing, so that you can effectively execute the ideas and concepts I discuss later on.

Form I

This one starts with the 4th finger and has a tricky position shift. Try to keep the line as legato as possible.

Form II

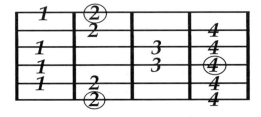

This is the simplest of the five forms, mainly because there are no shifts of the LH position.

Form III

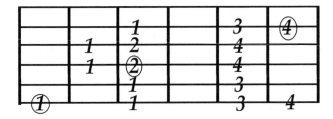

Stretch that first finger for this one! Pay attention to the other shifts as well, especially when coming back down.

Form IV

This one starts out easily, but the one shift on the 1st string is a big one. To keep a legato quality in the line, you'll have to make the shift quickly.

Form V

Okay, this one also starts on the 5th (A) string. The shift on the 1st string can be deceptive, so drill this one carefully.

As I said, there are many ways to practice these scales, but I will tell you about a few that have especially helped me. I hope they help you as well. In all cases, play the scale bottom to top and back without stopping, playing the top note only once. Have your metronome going and don't stop between scales!

1) Play one form chromatically all the way up the neck and back, starting on the lowest possible position (for Form I, that would be A). Go as high as you can on the neck. Do the same thing for all five forms. (By the way, this is a good way of learning any new scale or pattern.)

2) Pick any key and play all five forms in that key from the lowest to the highest possible position. You will find that you can fit all the forms for a given key on the fretboard. For example: starting in the key of F, you should play Form III in first position, followed by Form IV in fifth position, Form V in seventh position, Form I in tenth position and Form II in twelfth position. Got it? This one can be a brain bender, so take your time. It's very important to understand how the various forms link together, so spend at least a week doing this drill in all twelve keys.

3) Starting in any given key and with any form, play one major scale in each key going through the circle of fourths. The trick here is to find the <u>nearest available form</u> for the next key! You should start in the middle of the neck so you don't run out of room. If you do, just reposition for the next key.

4) This is a big one. Do exercise 2 above, going through the entire circle of fourths. In other words, all five forms in F, then all five forms in B flat, etc. When you're done with this one you will have played all 60 possible major scale forms on the fretboard in a single exercise. (With the metronome going, of course!)

Spend as much time on this material as you need before you go on. Trust me: if you have this stuff down COLD it will make the rest of the book that much easier. I can't emphasize this enough: intimate knowledge of major scales is essential in helping to learn the other scales AND in improvising generally.

MINOR SCALES

Minor scales come in three types: natural, harmonic, melodic. I am going to show the patterns for natural and melodic minor scales only, but I will include the pitches of the Harmonic Minor. First, let me show you the pitches for all three minor scales:

Natural Minor

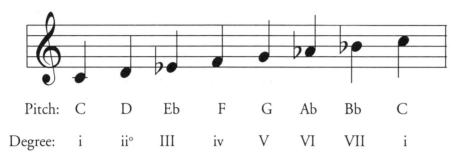

Pitch:	C	D	Eb	F	G	Ab	Bb	C
Degree:	i	ii°	III	iv	V	VI	VII	i

Harmonic Minor

Pitch:	C	D	Eb	F	G	Ab	B	C
Degree:	i	ii°	III	iv	V	VI	vii°	i

Melodic Minor

Pitch:	C	D	Eb	F	G	A	B	C
Degree:	i	ii°	III	iv	V	vi°	vii°	ii

Do you see the differences? The natural minor is just that: a minor scale in its pure form. Every natural minor scale is related, note for note, to the major scale that is a minor 3rd above it. In the case of C minor, that's Eb. In other words, the Eb major scale has the same notes as the C minor scale. Remember that relationship; it will be important to you later. The harmonic minor scale is identical except for the raised 7th. The minor 3rd space between the 6th and 7th has a nice "gypsy" quality. The melodic minor (also called the jazz minor) scale has a raised 6th and 7th. It can also be described as a major scale with a flatted 3rd, but that idea somewhat obscures its function. In music conservatories, the melodic minor is supposed to sound like a natural minor when descending, but we won't bother with that here. You should get this unique sound in your ear going in both directions. There are a lot of really cool altered scales that are based on the melodic minor, so we'll spend some extra time with it.

NATURAL MINOR

The natural minor scale is usable over minor chords that function as the vi in a major key (ex: Am in the key of C), with the possible exception of the Minor 7/9/11 family of chords. They're pretty easy to learn once you have the Major forms down.

Form I

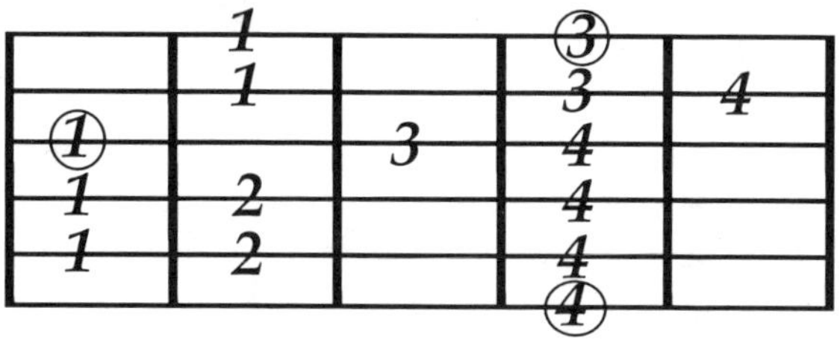

This one starts on the 4th finger. There's one shift between the 2nd and 3rd string. It's pretty simple.

Form II

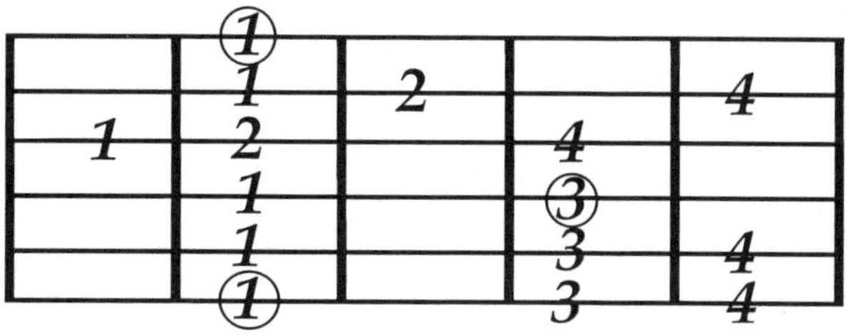

This is the form I use the most. Everything seems to lay easily under your fingers. Watch the shifts when descending.

Form III

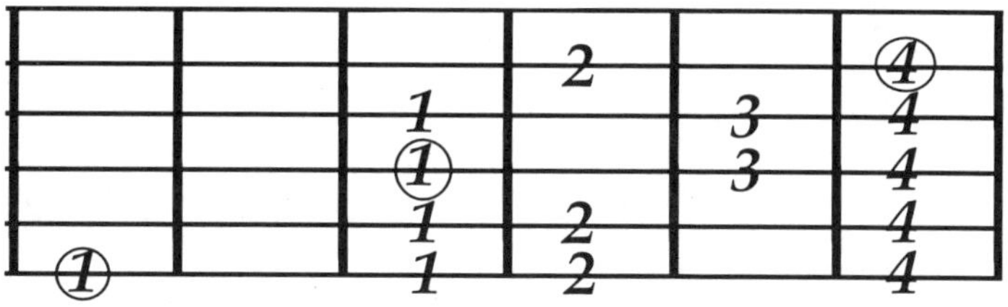

Starts off like the Form III Major. Other than that, this one is very simple.

Form IV

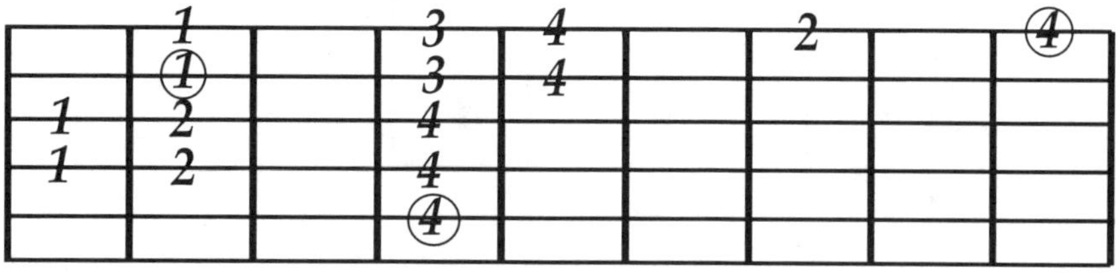

The big shift in this form is close to the one in the Form IV Major. It's a little odd in that the shift goes to the 2nd finger.

Form V

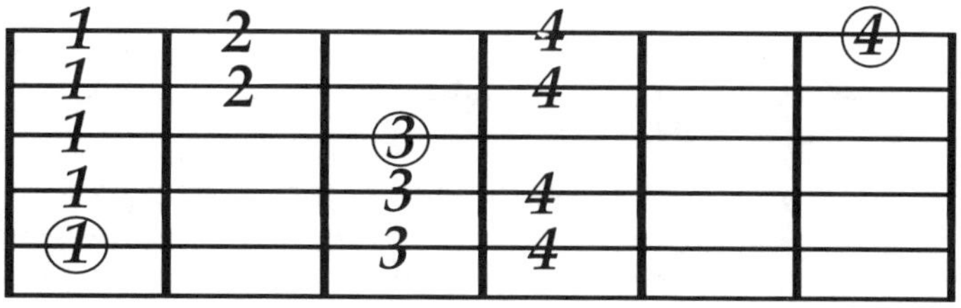

Here's another easy one. Your 4th finger gets a little workout at the top. Try to avoid slurring that shift.

MELODIC MINOR

This is an interesting scale. Sometimes called the "jazz minor," this scale has a curious minor/major sound to it. That makes it a perfect choice for playing over a Minor(Maj7) chord. It is also the basis for a whole host of altered scales in various keys. Just as the major scale is the basis for all the "standard" modes (Dorian, Lydian, etc.), the Melodic Minor scale is the basis for a whole family of altered modes that we'll discuss later. You should try to learn all these forms in such a way as to be able to interchange them easily.

Form I

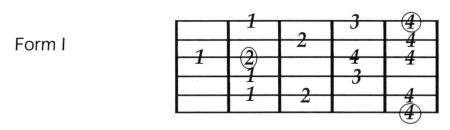

The shift on the 3rd string is designed to keep your LH in one position at all times. Remember this pattern as you will see it again with these scales.

Form II

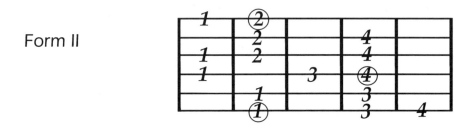

Notice the similarity with the Form II Major. This is what I mean by a major scale with a flattened third. It may help your fingerings if you think of it this way.

Form III

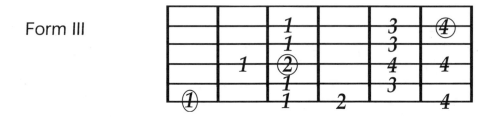

Here's the 1-2-4-4 pattern again. If you want, try 4-3-1-1 when descending. It may seem more natural to your LH.

Form IV

This one should seem pretty easy. Again, try 4-3-1-1 when descending on the 2nd string. The other fingering might slow down your natural momentum.

- 8 -

Form V

This one is pretty straightforward as well. Don't forget to grab the root with your 4th rather than 3rd finger when descending to the 3rd string.

Although I'm going to discuss this again later, I'll give you a little tidbit right now. Here's a neat little way you can solo using the Melodic Minor scale: whenever you see a dominant 7 chord with a flatted 5th, try using the scale based on a perfect 5th above the chord's root. Example: over a D9(b5), play an A Melodic Minor scale. You'll see that all the chord tones plus the altered note is in the scale. This can come in handy with tunes like "Take the A Train," etc. that use these chords.

A SHORT BREATHER...

Okay, where are you at this point? I've just dumped a ton of things on your head that you should practice. You should use the same drills for the minor forms that I showed you for the Major forms. Stick to the metronome, follow the guidelines I talked about earlier. This material may take you as long as a month or more to completely digest. Don't get impatient, just take your time and keep at it.

If you're sticking to these scales and using the fingering exercise as a warmup, by now you may notice your fingers becoming more responsive, your picking technique getting cleaner, your overall sound becoming more confident. It may be only a slight improvement or it may be dramatic. Either way, that's good. You've improved as a guitar player. Give yourself an "atta boy" (or "atta girl!").

One thing you may be thinking at this point is, "Okay. I know all these scales, but what do I do with them? How do I use them to improvise a jazz solo?" Well, you may be unaware of it, but you now have all the basic tools at hand to solo over a large majority of the jazz tunes you will ever hear! I am going to discuss this in a later section of the book entitled "Playing Over Changes," but let me tease you with some little ideas right now. Let's base our examples in the key of F Major.

Using an F Major scale as your palette, you can "paint" a variety of colors that fit over the following progression:

If you're not sure how to do that, just look at this little idea, using the same scale and same progression:

See what I mean? All I did was use notes from the F Major scale to construct a little 2-bar jazz solo! Record yourself playing the chord progression or have a friend play along for you, and try playing the above line. It sounds great, and from this you can experiment with other ideas that work over the same progression. Here's another little progression that will require a Major and a Melodic Minor scale:

If you're stuck as to what to do, remember that you can use a C major scale everywhere except for the D7b5 chord, where you need to use A melodic minor. Here's a sample lick that does exactly that:

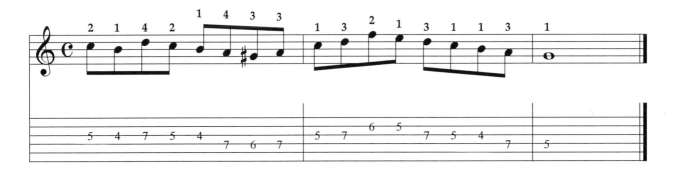

As with the other example, tape yourself playing the chords or have a friend accompany you. Use this to help you think of your own ideas. Have a little fun letting your creative juices flow after so much time spent running through those boring scales!

MODES

Okay. As I promised, we are now going to discuss modes. Modes were used in ancient Greek music instead of scales. They were also used in Gregorian chant and other Western music before the major-minor system that we have today. We can derive seven modes from the major scale alone (See, I told you it was important!). I'll explain what all the modes are, then I'll show you the fingerings and uses for the most necessary ones in jazz.

If you play a major scale from root to root, you get a very familiar sound. If, however, you play it starting and ending on another note, it sounds quite different. Here are the seven basic modes from the C major scale:

C Ionian

Pitch:	C	D	E	F	G	A	B	C
Degree:	1	2	3	4	5	6	7	1

D Dorian

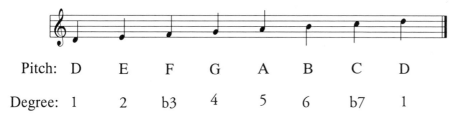

Pitch:	D	E	F	G	A	B	C	D
Degree:	1	2	b3	4	5	6	b7	1

E Phrygian

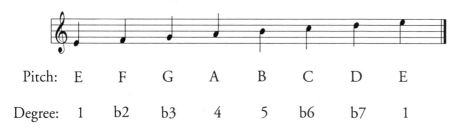

Pitch:	E	F	G	A	B	C	D	E
Degree:	1	b2	b3	4	5	b6	b7	1

F Lydian

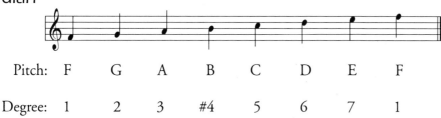

Pitch:	F	G	A	B	C	D	E	F
Degree:	1	2	3	#4	5	6	7	1

G Mixolydian

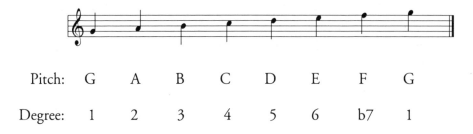

Pitch:	G	A	B	C	D	E	F	G
Degree:	1	2	3	4	5	6	b7	1

A Aeolian

Pitch:	A	B	C	D	E	F	G	A
Degree:	1	2	b3	4	5	b6	b7	1

B Locrian

Pitch	B	C	D	E	F	G	A	B
Degree	1	b2	b3	4	b5	b6	b7	1

All these modes have the same exact pitches as the C major scale, yet they just begin and end on different notes. Two of them you already know: the Ionian and the Aeolian. They are, of course, the Major and Natural Minor scales. The other modes are also used in jazz improvisation. I will emphasize the two most important ones first: the Dorian and the Mixolydian. I say "most important" because they are the most used and will allow you the greatest mileage in getting through a variety of situations.

DORIAN MODES

The Dorian mode is used in soloing over the Minor 7 family of chords. This includes Min 7, Min 9, Min 11, Min 7(add 13), etc. You may notice that it is identical to the minor scale except for the 6th degree, which is a half step higher. This pitch, also called the 13th, allows for a nice leading tone that emphasizes the 7th, giving the mode a hipper sound. The late great Charlie Christian used this note in his solos.

I have organized the fingerings into 5 forms like the other scales. This routine should be familiar to you by now, so I'll skip the commentary. Here you go:

Form I

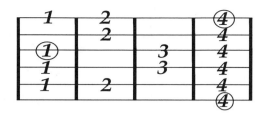

Form II

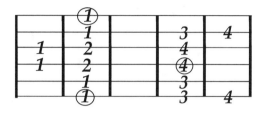

Form III

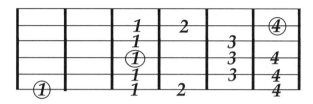

Form IV

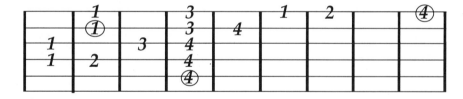

Form V

You should use the same practice routines as for the other scales to completely ingrain these fingerings in your reflex memory. Don't get confused by the similarity to the minor scale!

MIXOLYDIAN MODES

These modes are sometimes called "Dominant 7th Scales." There's good reason for that. You will notice that they are like major scales except for the presence of the flat 7th. The Mixolydian is used for any dominant 7th chord (7, 9, 11, 13, 9sus4, etc.). As such, they are extremely useful. Spend some extra time with these; you will find the need for them quite often.

Form I

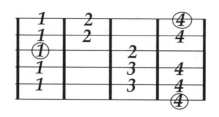

Form II

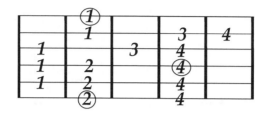

Form III

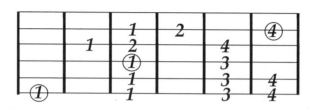

Form IV

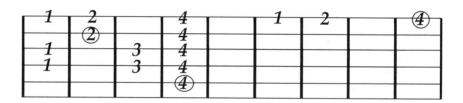

Form V

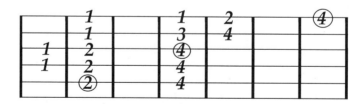

These are used throughout the blues and over any dominant chord. Since jazz is full of such chords, you will rely on the Mixolydian quite a bit.

The other modes fall under the category of altered scales, since the chords they fit over are "altered chords" so we will deal with them later. First, let's look at ways we can use the Dorian and Mixolydian, and add to what we already know. Let's go back to this chord progression:

Over the Gmin7 chord, you want to use G Dorian, while over C7, you need C Mixolydian. Play these two modes in that order in any position or form you wish. Make the position shifts natural. Your line should sound like this:

Over the Fmaj7 chord we would of course use the F Major scale. So in the above progression, you would use G Dorian, C Mixolydian and F Major. Do you notice anything in common with these scales? Yep, that's right: they all have the same pitches! G Dorian and C Mixolydian are both derived from F Major. Go back to the example on F Major and analyze it. Sure enough, those modes are represented in the line.

Now before you write me a nasty letter complaining how I made you learn all these modes when you could have just used one scale, remember that not all chord progressions are that simple. Check this one out:

This is based on a familiar jazz standard. Try and figure out what modes and scales you need to solo over these chords. Record yourself playing these changes over and over and then experiment. Try the modes ascending and descending; in half, quarter or eighth notes; basically any combination you can think of. If you get stuck, here's an example that might stimulate your ideas:

Look carefully at the line. There are several mode combinations that can be grouped under one major scale. If you noticed that earlier, you're ahead of the game. If you still don't see it, don't worry. We'll look at that aspect again later.

Spend time practicing these modes in conjunction with the major and minor scales: Here's a good practice routine:

1) Play C Major in all 5 forms.

2) Play C Natural Minor in all 5 forms.

3) Play C Melodic Minor in all 5 forms.

4) Play C Dorian in all 5 forms.

5) Play C Mixolydian in all 5 forms.

6) Go to the key of F and repeat 1 through 5. Continue through the circle of 4ths until you return to C.

This is a long one, but if you go through it, you will end up with a firm grounding in the jazz scale vocabulary. You'll need it, because we're about to enter the realm of altered harmonies. Hang on!

DIMINISHED SCALES

Strictly speaking, the diminished arpeggio is a succession of minor thirds. But there is a scale that connects those pitches together. It contains the notes of a diminished 7th chord (1,b3,b5, bb7), with a passing tone a half step below each. It has a unique whole step/half step structure. This scale repeats itself every minor third, which means that there are actually only three diminished scales (based on C, D and E)! Before you get too confused about that, let's look at the basic diminished scale:

C Diminished (Cdim. or C °)

Pitch:	C	D	Eb	F	Gb	Ab	A	B	C
Degree:	1	2	b3	4	b5	b6	6(bb7)	7	1

The diminished scale has a close cousin that is constructed on the half step/whole step model. It also repeats itself every minor third and, yes, there are only three of these as well (C, D and E). In the interest of simplicity, I have called it the "altered dominant" scale. It looks like this:

C Altered Dominant

Pitch:	C	Db	Eb	E	Gb	Ab	A	B	C
Degree:	1	b2	b3	3	b5	5	6	b7	1

I call this scale "altered dominant" because it contains all the notes of a dominant 7th chord (1, 3, 5, b7) as well a host of color tones that include the b9, #9, #11, and 13. Strictly speaking, this isn't a diminished scale, but you will soon see why I include it in this section.

The diminished scale is used over all diminished chords as well as certain dominant 7th chords when they are used in turnarounds or in passing. The altered dominant is used over a number of "altered" chords, specifically, dom. 7th with any extended color tone except for the #5: C7b5, C7b9, C7#9, C7(b9#11), C7(#9#11), C13b9, C13#11, etc. Obviously, it is a very powerful improvisational tool!

You may notice that these scales have eight notes rather than seven. That length makes it easy to continue into the next octave in a rhythmically smooth fashion. Their fingerings are similar, almost identical, in fact. They can also be repeated every three frets on the neck (a distinction shared by all diminished chord or scale forms). This means that the C diminished is also the Eb, Gb and A diminished. The same goes for the Altered Dominant. This makes it easy to use these scale forms when soloing over passing chords — they're always right under your fingers!

For each scale, I will show you one basic scale shape, then an "extended" scale shape that can get you all the way up or down the neck. Here is the diminished scale:

Here is the "extended" diminished scale form:

Notice how the patterns interlock with each other. If you remember the basic 1-2-4-4 pattern, you will always get a diminished sound. If you wish, on the extended form you can play 4-3-1-1 when descending. It sometimes flows better.

DIMINISHED ARPEGGIO

If you eliminate the half step passing tones, you get a four-note diminished arpeggio. Here are two simple fingerings that will prove useful for you:

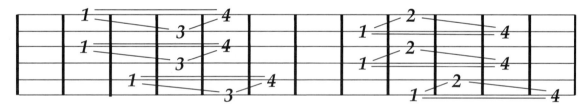

As you learn these patterns, try to visualize a series of interlocking triangles on the fretboard. It helps in navigation, since there is no real key center your ear can hear and gravitate toward.

Now, as I said, the Altered Dominant scale is nearly identical to the Diminished fingering. In fact, all you have to do is add one note on bottom and take one away up top! It is also repeated every three frets. Here is the basic scale pattern:

The fingering is the same as a diminished scale located one fret higher. Do you see it? That means, for instance, that the F Altered Dominant scale is basically the same as the F# Diminished scale. Think about that for a minute. You have at your disposal a musical tool that can be used over 4 diminished chords and at least 28 different altered dominant chords! Needless to say, you should internalize these forms diligently. With that in mind, can you figure out an extended altered dominant scale form? It will also be nearly identical to the diminished. Here is one that you will recognize:

[fretboard diagram]

You can also extend the bottom notes on the 6th string like so:

[fretboard diagram]

As for an Altered Dominant arpeggio, just be lazy. Use the diminished arpeggio form. You'll get the 1, b3, b5, and 6 (13). Now try the same pattern a fret higher. You'll get an arpeggio that includes the b9, 3, 5 and b7. What a bargain! Here's a little drill that makes use of that aspect. Play it over a C7#9 chord:

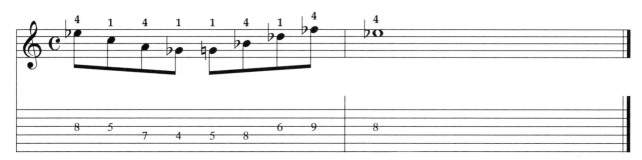

All you have to do is play the diminished arpeggio form descending from the C, then shift up one fret and play the same thing going back up. This drill is good for your ear.

Take some time studying these forms. Learn them in all keys (that should be easy!), and get used to their sounds. There is a subtle difference in sound between the diminished and altered dominant. You should do the same kind of practice drill as you did for the other scales we have looked at so far. Play them over prerecorded rhythm chords to get used to using them. If you want to hear a splendid example of these forms in actual use, listen to John Coltrane. He was a real pioneer of the diminished/altered sound in jazz improvisation.

Here's a good exercise that will help you get the patterns under your fingers. You should memorize the fingering, then learn it in all keys:

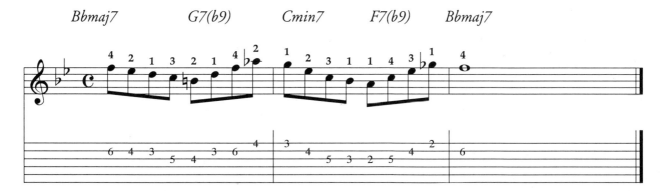

- 19 -

As I said, diminished chords are used in passing and in "turnarounds." That is a jazz musician's term for a cadence at the end of a phrase. Here is a common progression involving diminished chords:

Play this progression a few times. Do you hear how the diminished chords "lead" your ear toward the next chord? For that reason they are known as "leading tone" chords. Here is an example of a line you can play over this progression:

If you analyze the line, you will see the scales and modes we have talked about earlier. F Major, G Dorian, A Mixolydian, etc. Let's have some fun and make the A7 an altered chord. Look how the line can change:

The A altered dominant scale to the rescue! I hope you like the sound in this scale. I should caution you, however. If the altered chord resolves to a minor chord like the above example, you might be better off not using this scale. The 6th of the scale corresponds to a major 3rd of the next chord, making A7alt.->DMaj a better opportunity. It can be a hip sound if you're daring enough, though. If you encounter an altered 7th going to a minor (and you will), a more effective choice would be the Diminished/Wholetone scale, but we're getting ahead of ourselves! Other things first.

WHOLETONE SCALES

It is said that Wes Montgomery once told George Benson that there were only four types of scales to worry about: major, minor, augmented and diminished. Everything else comes from that. Well, I'm hardly in a position to disagree with Wes, and in fact I heartily agree with him. Everything you have seen in this book so far is a derivative of either major, minor, or diminished. Well, here's the fourth "food group" of scales: augmented.

The augmented triad contains 1, 3 and #5. In the key of C, that would be C, E and G#. The scale that corresponds to this chord is called the "wholetone" scale because it is made up entirely of whole steps. Here it is:

C Wholetone

Pitch:	C	D	E	F#	G#	Bb	C
Degree:	1	2	3	#4	#5	b7	1

Like the diminished scale family, the wholetone family has some unique properties. It is also a "rootless" scale, that is, any note of the scale could be its root. Since there are six pitches in the scale, and there are only twelve pitches in Western harmony, that means that there are only two wholetone scales (C and C#)! On the fretboard, the wholetone fingerings can be repeated every other fret, making learning scale patterns a snap.

Notice also that the wholetone scale contains the 1, 3 and b7, which are the essential notes of a dominant 7th chord. The addition of the 2, #4 and #5 allow you to use this over certain types of altered dominants. We'll look at an example of this shortly. Here's a basic wholetone scale pattern:

I guess you see how you need to stretch your first finger to make the notes come out smoothly. Here is an "extended" wholetone scale form:

It helps me to visualize staggered rows of bricks on a wall when I play this pattern. Watch out for the change in the pattern between the 2nd and 3rd strings. As I said, this pattern can be repeated every other fret. Try the basic scale shape starting on the 1st, 3rd, 5th, 7th frets, etc. You will hear the notes being repeated.

- 21 -

The wholetone scale is used over most types of augmented chords as well as some altered dominants, i.e., 7b5, 9#5, 9#11, etc. Here is a good practice pattern:

Try this pattern over a Caug7 (also written C7+), as well as some of the other chords I mentioned. Here is a progression that will call for a wholetone scale:

Construct a line that uses C major, D wholetone, D dorian, G wholetone and C major. If you think, you can reduce the needed scales to three. If you get stuck, here's an example:

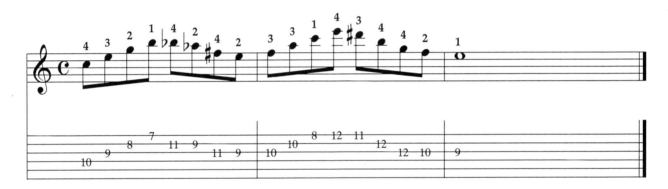

What are the three scales that can get you through this progression? C major, C wholetone and G wholetone. Remember, D dorian has the same pitches as C major, as does D wholetone with C wholetone. If you try to boil these scale choices down whenever you can, you will make it easier to construct a good solo. We'll look at more examples later.

DIMINISHED/WHOLETONE SCALE

Remember earlier when we looked at the Altered Dominant and I mentioned that it was better for dominant chords resolving to major chords? Well, here's the best choice for soloing over dominants that resolve to MINORS. Just as its name implies, the Diminished/Wholetone scale is part diminished, part wholetone. Let's take a look:

C Diminished/Wholetone

Pitch:	C	Db	Eb	E	F#/Gb	G#/Ab	Bb	C
Degree:	1	b2	b3	3	#4/b5	#5/b6	b7	1

- 22 -

Notice that the first half of the scale is more like the altered dominant (half/whole instead of whole/half), but this is what everyone calls this scale, so I guess I'll just conform! Anyway, look at the pitches. Do you notice the b6? If this was a dominant chord, that would be the minor third of the chord we would be resolving to. In other words, if I were soloing over a C7b9 going to Fmin, I could have the Ab note sounding to get a bluesy augmented feel over the C7. When it goes to the Fmin, there would be a nice release of tension.

Okay, here's a dirty little secret: remember when I told you the Melodic Minor could be used to form altered modes? Well, this is one. Start a melodic minor on the 7th degree and you have a diminished wholetone scale. Look at the scale again. Aren't those also the notes of a Db melodic minor scale? They sure are! So go back to the melodic minors and work out new patterns, starting and ending on the 7th scale degree. Create five forms and write them out just like I have them. Practice them like you would any other scale. You'll be intrigued by the sound. In addition to the five basic forms, here is an extended fingering for the diminished/wholetone scale:

As an interesting drill, play several alt.V -> I progressions in minor keys (for example, a G7#9 going to Cm). Tape your playing. Then play the appropriate dim./w.t. over the V, and a minor over the I. See if you can work out some nice lines from this exercise.

MODES II

This is a good point at which to discuss two other modes that are used in jazz playing: Lydian and Locrian. I didn't talk about them earlier because I wanted you to concentrate on the most important (and most frequently used) modes in order to get started. You've come along quite a bit now, so I think it's time we looked at these. Like the other modes, these are based on the Major scale. Let's look at the Lydian mode first.

LYDIAN MODES

Go back to my earlier discussion of modes and you will see that the Lydian is simply a major scale starting and ending on the 4th degree. As an example, I showed the F Lydian Mode. Another way of describing them is to say that they are major scales with a raised 4th. Let me show you an example in C:

C LYDIAN MODE

Pitch:	C	D	E	F#	G	A	B	C
Degree:	1	2	3	#4	5	6	7	1

Try playing this mode, bottom to top. It has a very Major sound, yet somehow more unresolved. That's because the 4th degree has been replaced by a leading tone that points your ear toward the 5th (G). This mode is used over any kind of Major (#11) chord or in place of the Major scale when the chord in question is anything but the tonic. For example: if you were soloing in the key of Ab Major, and had to play over a Dbmaj7 (the IV chord), you would want to use Db Lydian rather than Db Major.

Here are the five forms for the Lydian mode:

Form I

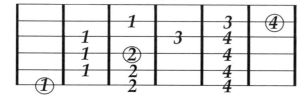

Form II

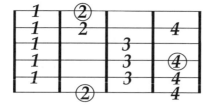

Form III

Form IV

Form V

Of course, you should use the same drills to learn these forms as with any of the other scales in this book. This would also be a good time to double check your picking technique and hand positioning. It never hurts to review the basics!

Lydian b7

There is an altered version of the Lydian known as the Lydian b7. As you might have guessed, it is a Lydian mode with a lowered 7th degree. The Lydian b7 is quite handy for playing over most dom7 or dom9 chords that have the b5/#11. For the fingerings to this version, go back to the above five forms, flat all the sevenths and work out a new fingering pattern.

LOCRIAN MODES

The Locrian mode starts on the 7th degree of the major scale. It is also known as the "half-diminished" scale because it is used almost exclusively over the half-diminished family of chords. Before we look at this mode, we should discuss this chord family and its' function.

In music conservatories, you would be told that the half-diminished 7 chord was composed of 1, b3, b5, b7. It is called "half" diminished because the 7th is not itself a diminished interval (like the regular diminished chord). This chord is called a "leading tone" chord because each of the notes leads to some kind of resolution. Typically, the half-diminished chord resolves up a half step to a major chord in a major key, while it functions as the II (subdominant) in a minor key. It isn't often encountered.

In jazz, however, the half-diminished chord occurs all the time. Its first widespread use was by Dizzy Gillespie, who discovered it as a "minor 6th chord with the 6th in the bass," and named it the min7(b5) chord. That name has stuck. To this day, you can almost tell if a musician has a jazz or classical background by what he calls this particular chord! At any rate, the min7(b5) chord is found much more often in jazz than in classical music. You will see it used most often as the II chord in minor keys, for example: Bmin7(b5) -> E7(b9) -> A min. Let's look at the locrian mode in C:

C Locrian

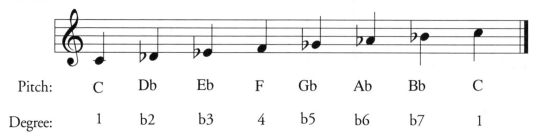

Pitch:	C	Db	Eb	F	Gb	Ab	Bb	C
Degree:	1	b2	b3	4	b5	b6	b7	1

You can see that in addition to the chord tones there are some other notes (b2, b6) that will yield some nice harmonic colors. Try to play this mode bottom to top to get the sound in your ear. It does have a slightly "diminished" quality. Here are the five forms for the Locrian mode:

Form I

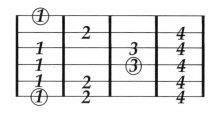

Form II

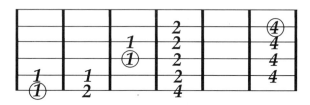

Form III

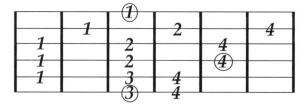

Form IV

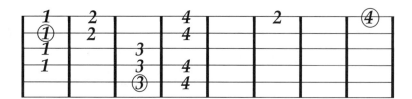

Form V

Here is a good exercise drill for the Locrian mode: Pick a minor II->V->I progression, like Amin7(b5)->D7b9->Gmin7. Record those changes. Then play the following patterns: A locrian, D diminished/wholetone, G dorian. Use common tones to connect the patterns together, like this:

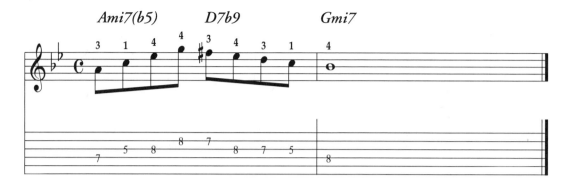

Try this exercise in all keys and positions. It's an important progression to know, as it occurs frequently in jazz.

SUPER LOCRIAN

There is a variation of the Locrian mode known as the Super Locrian. The only difference is that it has a raised second degree (#2). That would make the C Super Locrian look like this: C - D - Eb - F - Gb - Ab - Bb - C. It's sort of a natural minor scale with a flatted 5th, or a "minor/wholetone" scale. Work out five patterns based on the regular Locrian for this mode. (Hint: also try working out patterns from the Natural Minor and see if they come out the same!)

The super Locrian is useful when you encounter a IImin7(b5) -> V7b9 -> Imaj7. It happens, so don't be surprised when you see it! There are other uses for the Super Locrian as well. See if you can figure some of them out!

PENTATONICS AND THE BLUES

This may surprise some guitar players. The material that most books put at the beginning I save for the end. Well, I believe that as a guitar player, you should understand regular diatonic harmony first, and only then learn the "rule breaking" material. That's so you can understand how blues forms are derived and what other scales you can use in a blues progression. So many players start out with just blues scales and end up in a rut, both technically and musically. I'm trying to get you to think like a MUSICIAN and not just a guitar player.

Nevertheless, this book would be woefully incomplete without a look at Blues forms. Blues music is the basis for jazz, and you should know about it. This section will also deal with the Bebop scales, which I consider to be close relatives of Blues scales.

PENTATONIC SCALES

First, let's deal with the Major Pentatonic scale. As its name implies, it has five notes. They are as follows:

C Major Pentatonic

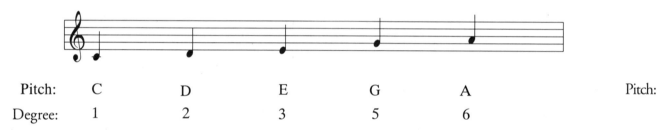

Pitch:	C	D	E	G	A
Degree:	1	2	3	5	6

It's a very simple musical construction based on a C Major chord. You probably already know some licks that use this scale. Here's the minor version:

C Minor Pentatonic

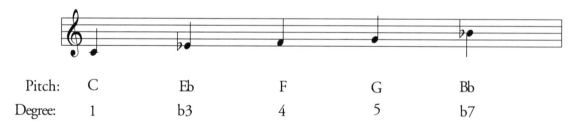

Pitch:	C	Eb	F	G	Bb
Degree:	1	b3	4	5	b7

You can see how this outlines a min7 chord. The b3 and b7 are known as "blue notes," some of the earliest used notes in jazz improvisation. Listen to recordings of early Louis Armstrong, King Oliver or Jelly Roll Morton to hear these notes as they were originally used. It may sound square to our ears, but it was downright "avant-garde" to listeners in 1924!

Just as a major scale corresponds note-for-note with its relative minor, the major and relative minor pentatonics also match up (i.e., C major with A minor, F major with D minor, etc.). For that reason, I will just give you five forms and call them "Pentatonic":

Form I

Form II

Form III

Form IV

Form V

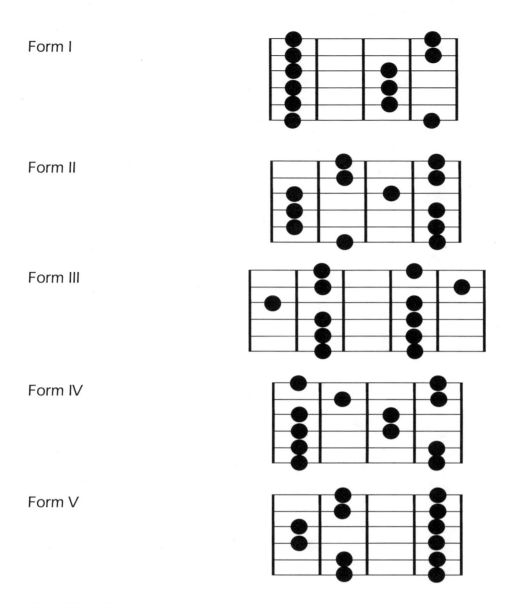

BLUES SCALES

The only difference between Blues and Pentatonic scales is one note. In the Major it's the b3, while in minor it's the b5. Let's look at both blues scales:

C Major Blues

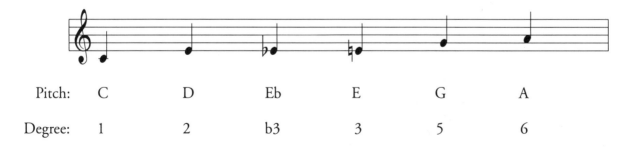

Pitch:	C	D	Eb	E	G	A
Degree:	1	2	b3	3	5	6

C Minor Blues

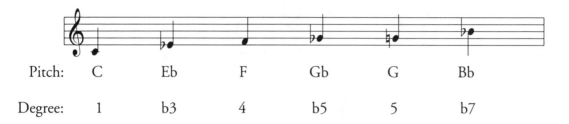

Pitch:	C	Eb	F	Gb	G	Bb
Degree:	1	b3	4	b5	5	b7

You just need to play these scales as written to hear the "bluesy" quality they have. They have the same major/relative minor relationship as the pentatonics, so I will show you just the five moveable forms and let you figure out their Major or Minor context. You should be getting pretty good at this by now!

Form I

Form II

Form III

Form IV

Form V

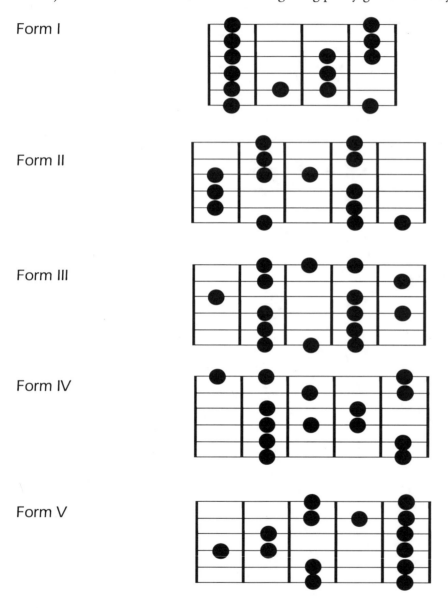

Okay, I'm going to talk in depth about Blues song forms in the next section of this book, but let me give you a quick example of how to use the scales. Here's a little "mini-blues" progression:

Using all Major blues scales (Cmajor blues, F major blues, C major blues), we get a line something like this:

Experiment with this progression. Play the chords on tape, then use these scales with different rhythms, starting notes, etc. Also try these blues scale combinations: Cmaj/Cmin/Cmaj;Cmin/Fmaj/Cmin;Cmaj/Fmin/Cmaj;Cmin/Fmin/Cmin. Also substitute corresponding pentatonics in some places. Some sound better than others, but they are all worth studying.

Bebop Scales

The Bebop era of the 40's and early 50's was one of the most revolutionary periods in American musical history. The entire face of jazz changed permanently from a type of "popular" music to a true art form. The two most important figures in this transformation were alto saxophonist Charlie Parker (1920-1955) and trumpeter Dizzy Gillespie (1924-1993). No jazz record collection is complete without some of their offerings.

One of the most important contributions they made was in the area of improvisation. They took the upper added tones of the chords (the 9th, 11th, 13th) and emphasized them in their solos. They also developed new scales, based on the Mixolydian and Major scales, that allowed all the chord tones to fall on downbeats and let the soloist connect long melodic lines together without needing to skip notes or beats. This demanded a degree of virtuosity to understand (let alone play), but it has deeply affected every jazz musician since.

Eventually, their method of using these scales was codified by jazz historians and educators and given the name "bebop" scales. Let's first look at the Bebop Dominant scale. It's basically a Mixolydian with a natural 7th degree added.

C Bebop Dominant

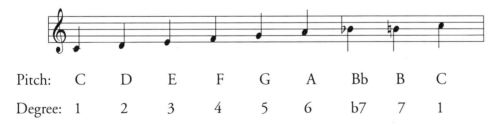

Pitch:	C	D	E	F	G	A	Bb	B	C
Degree:	1	2	3	4	5	6	b7	7	1

For the fingerings for this scale, go back to the Mixolydian forms and add the natural 7th. You will have the five forms for the Bebop Dominant. This scale is used wherever the Mixolydian or Major Blues scales are used. Try it and you'll hear the unique sound it yields. Here is a little example of how it works:

Did you notice how I used the F bebop dominant and connected the line back to the C7 chord? That's how easy these scales are to use. You can play without stopping if you keep using chord tones on downbeats. That's how the bebop masters could play such long phrases!

The Bebop Major scale is a Major scale with an added b6. Just as in the Dominant version, this scale has the added note so that the chord tones fall on downbeats. Here is the scale:

C Bebop Major

Pitch:	C	D	E	F	G	Ab	A	B	C
Degree:	1	2	3	4	5	b6	6	7	1

Again, like the Dominant version, you can figure out all the fingering patterns yourself. Go back to the Major scale patterns and add the b6. It should be simple to do. You can use the Bebop Major in place of the Major scale. Here is an example:

LICKS

This section of the book begins to put into practice all the things you have been learning up to now. We will look at examples of soloing over various types of chord changes and patterns, as well as how to analyze chord progressions to find the simplest way to construct a good line. First, we'll take a look at some easy "licks" that you can put in your little bag of tricks whenever you need them. Here they are:

MAJOR LICKS

F Major

- 33 -

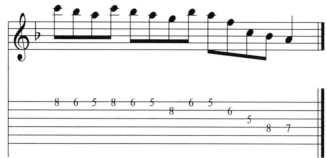

MAJOR 7 LICKS

C Major 7

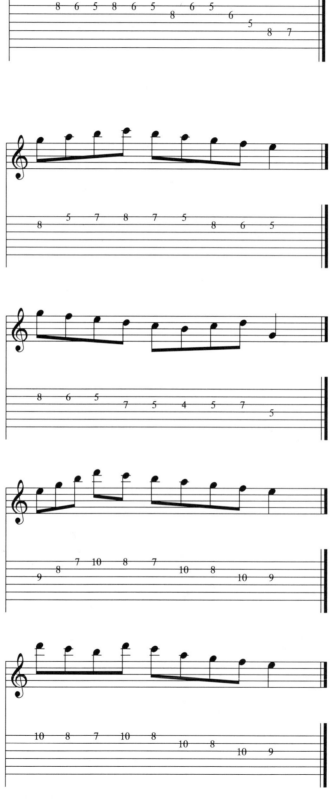

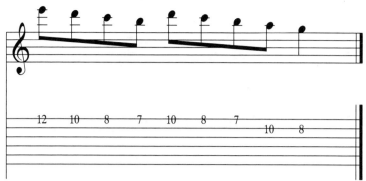

DOMINANT LICKS

Bb7

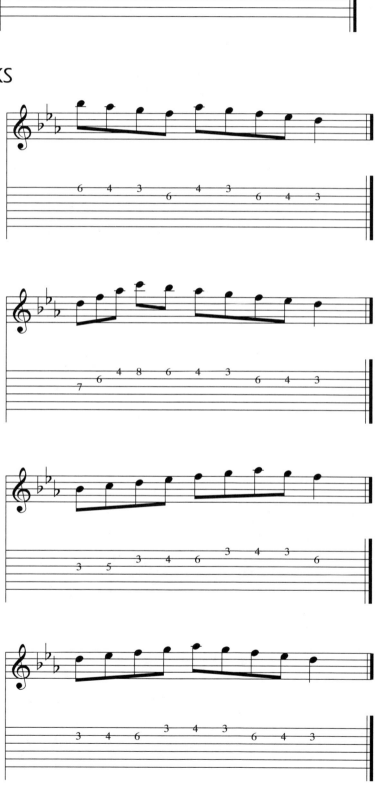

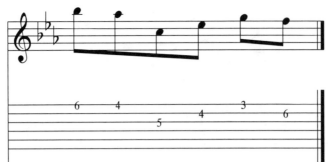

MINOR LICKS

A Minor

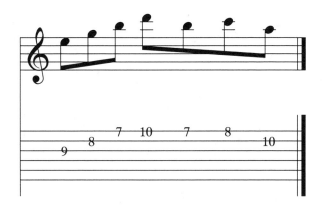

BEBOP LICKS

C7

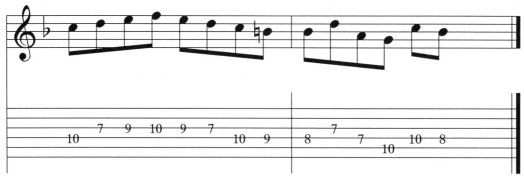

BLUES LICKS
A Minor

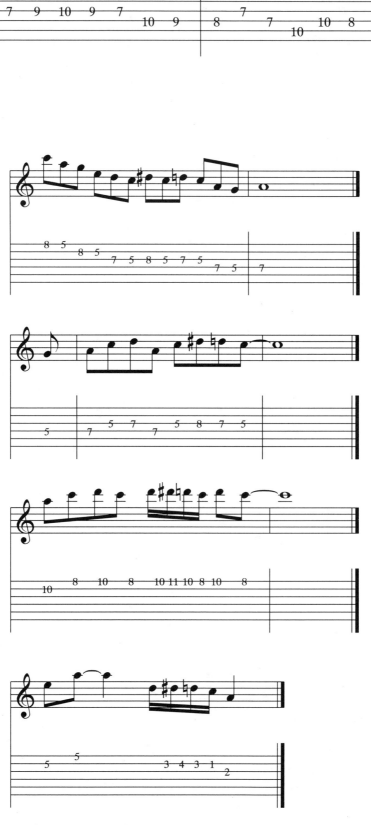

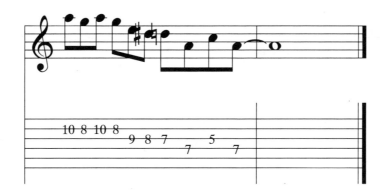

ALTERED DOMINANT LICKS

C7 (#9)

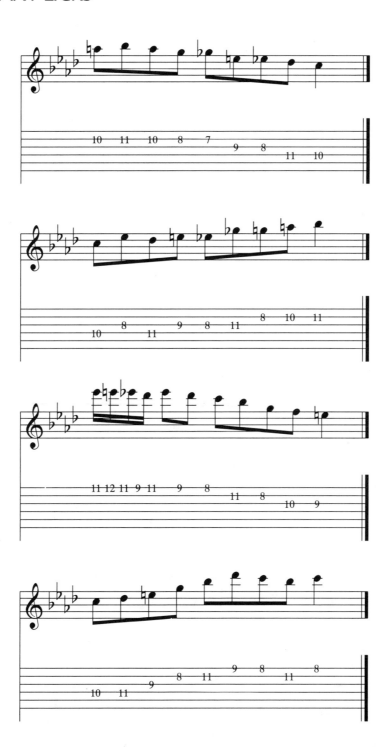

DIMINISHED LICKS

C Dim. 7

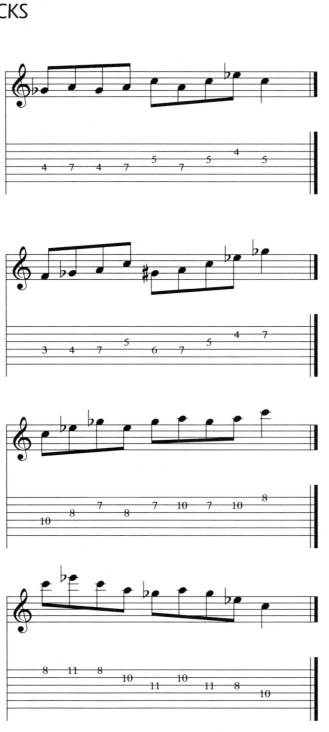

WHOLETONE (AUGMENTED) LICKS

G7+

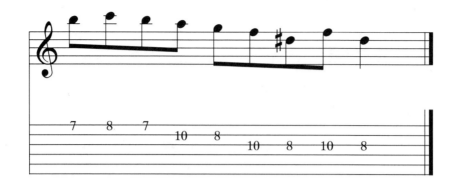

NOTE: I should mention that it would be advisable for you to work these licks out in all keys. I can't do all of your homework, you know!

TURNAROUNDS

As I mentioned before, jazz players refer to the cadence at the end of a phrase as a "turnaround." It can best be described as the way music ends one paragraph and starts another. There are a number of standardized turnaround patterns. Here are a few, each with an example lick you can try (without tab this time). They're all in the key of C, but again, learn them in all keys.

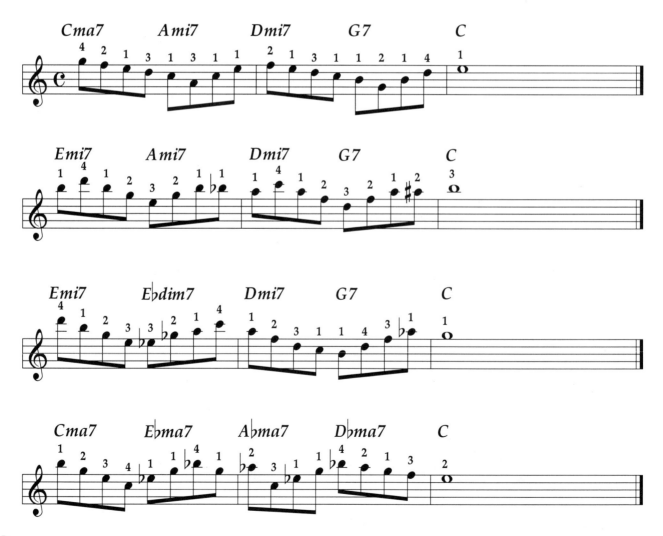

CHEAP TRICKS

Finally, I couldn't resist the temptation to throw in a few "cheap tricks." They're not tricks, really. These examples are just designed to take advantage of the peculiarities of the guitar. In some cases, they sacrifice musicality for technical ease, which earns the title of "cheap." But don't feel guilty about learning them. All instruments have certain properties which allow for certain kinds of playing. For example, trumpeters may play a lot of arpeggiated runs in thirds, while saxophonists blow long, extremely chromatic lines. That's because it's easy on their instrument. So, here are some things that will be technically easy for YOU to play, while making the horn players' mouths drop open (hopefully)!

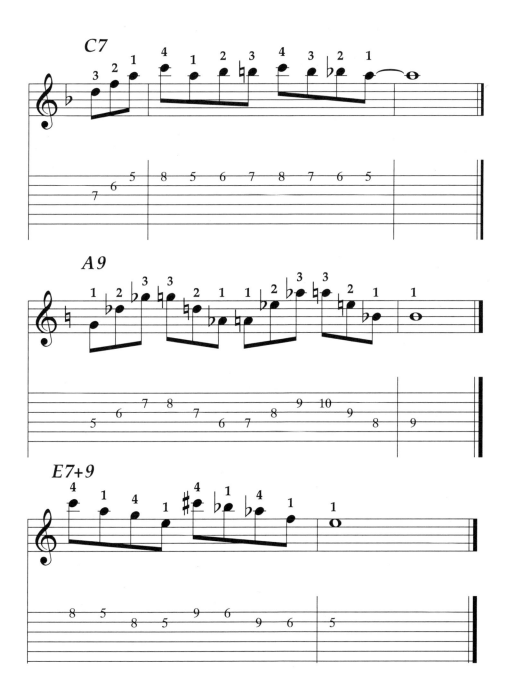

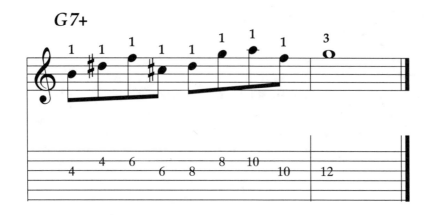

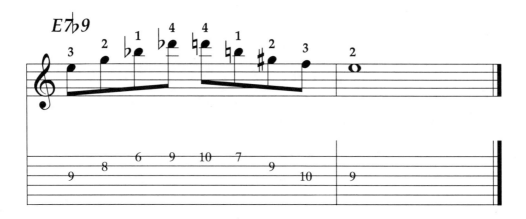

Okay, enough cheap guitar licks. Now it's time to try to make some musical sense of this. Here are some real-life musical examples to which you can apply all this stuff!

PLAYING OVER CHANGES

Now that you are familiar with the basic ingredients of jazz improvisation and have been exposed to some handy little shortcuts that will help your playing, it's time to look at some realistic musical situations that you will be faced with as a jazz guitar soloist. There are sets of common jazz progressions which the musician "in the know" should have thoroughly internalized. It's not uncommon at a jazz gig for a band leader to call a tune that the musicians have to play completely from memory. Therefore, you should know the following chord changes quite well. Spend some time in this section of the book; it could wind up landing you a job!

BLUES

The blues is the grandfather of jazz and almost every other form of American music. It follows that the most common jazz form you will encounter will be the blues. I have broken all the forms of blues down to four basic categories: traditional, modern, major and minor. They all share a 12-bar form. Here is the traditional 12-bar blues in the key of F:

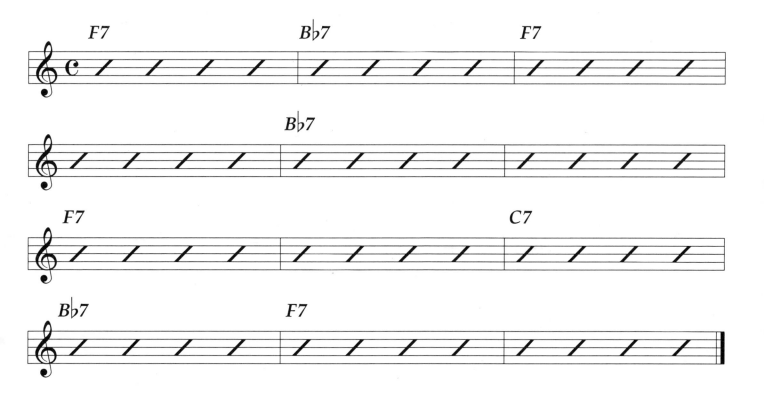

Here is a more modern version. Notice how it ends in a II-V-I instead of the V-IV-I like the traditional blues. There are also some additional passing chords:

- 45 -

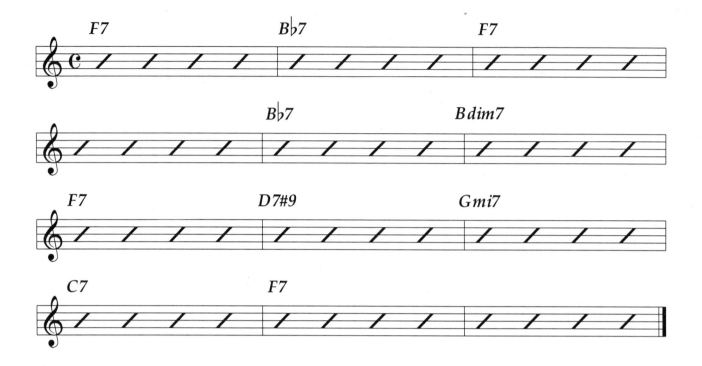

This is what I call a "major" blues. It uses the same form, but the tonic is a Major 7 rather than a dominant chord. This gives it a much different quality:

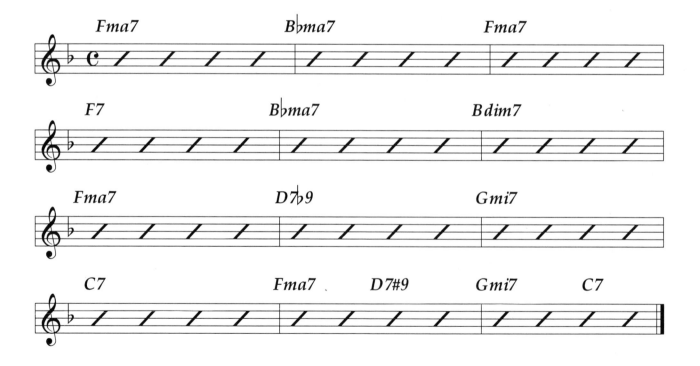

Here is the "minor" blues. The form is still 12 bars long, but the chord progression is slightly different. Just for a change of pace I'll put it in C minor:

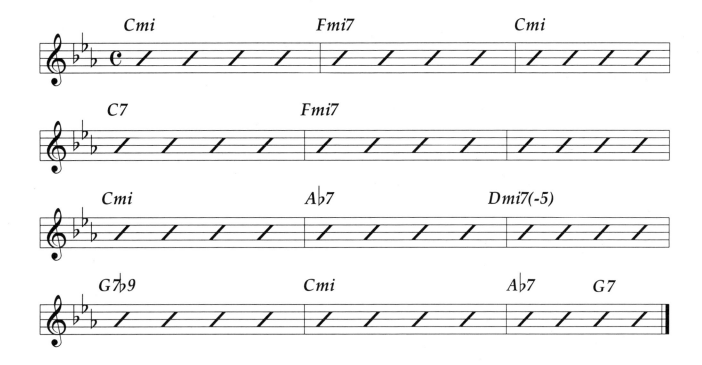

RHYTHM CHANGES

You may have heard this term before and wondered what it meant. It is not just another term for chord changes, but refers to a specific chord progression. The chords are based on the George Gershwin tune "I Got Rhythm," a classic song and the basis for almost as many jazz tunes as the blues. This progression is a 32-bar AABA form in the key of Bb:

The same changes as used in...

I Got Rhythm (Traditional)

Here is a more modernized variation with the same changes as used in:

I Got Rhythm (Modern)

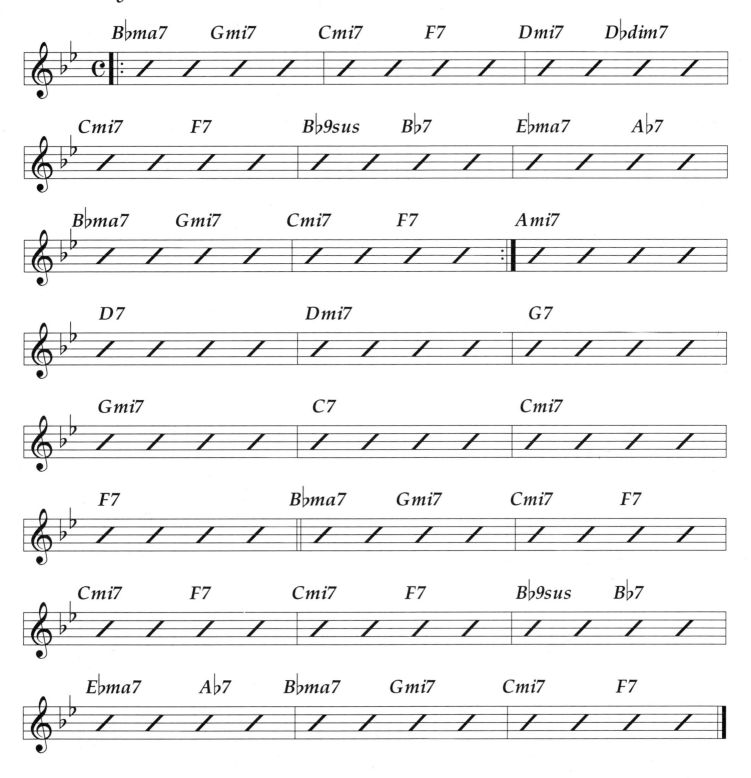

NOTE: Just because I gave you these examples in only one key, don't be surprised to see them in others. You should know these progressions in as many keys as possible.

OTHER CHANGES

While the Blues and Rhythm changes are the most common forms in jazz, there are others you should know. They are based on popular songs and have been used as a basis for others. Here are a few:

The same changes as used in...

Back Home Again in Indiana

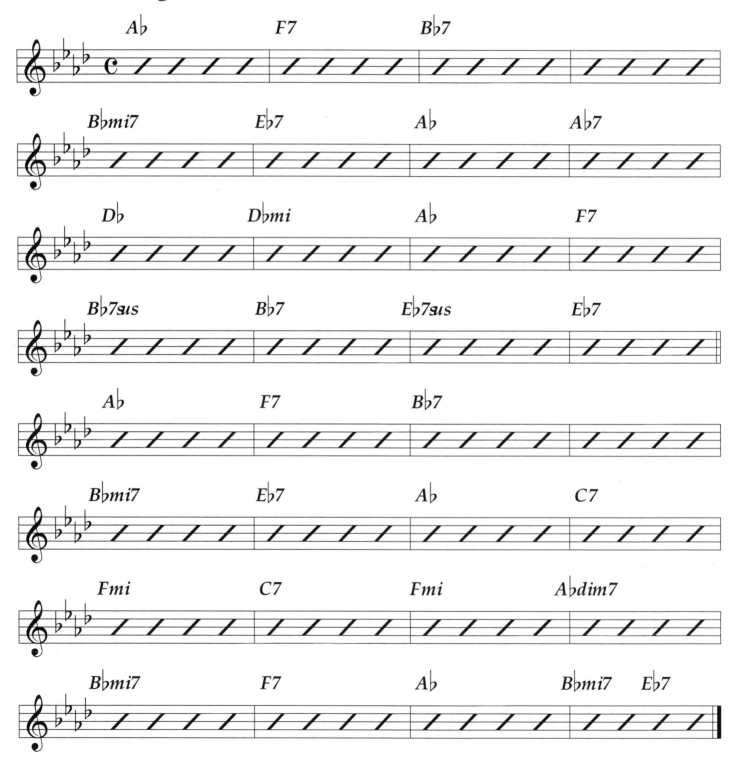

The same changes as used in...

How High the Moon

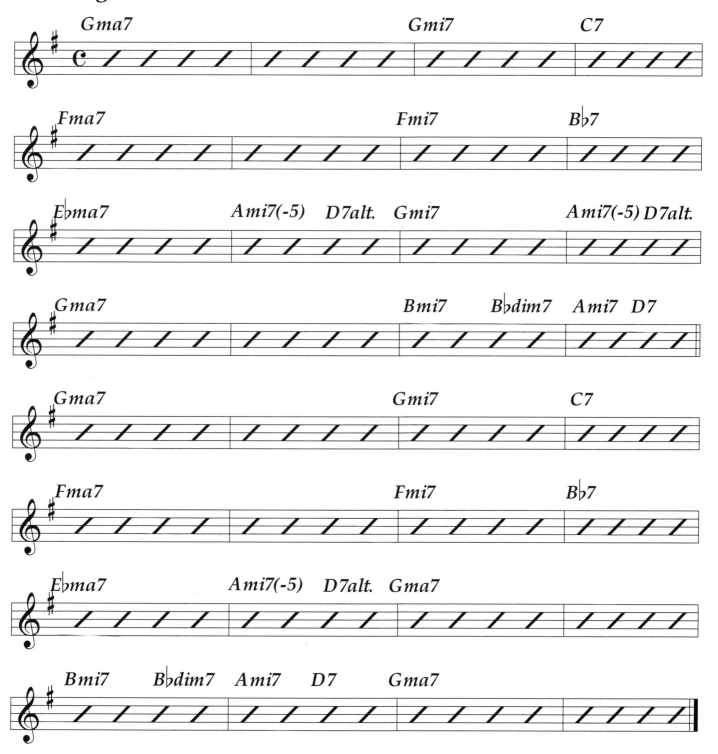

The same changes as used in...

Honeysuckle Rose

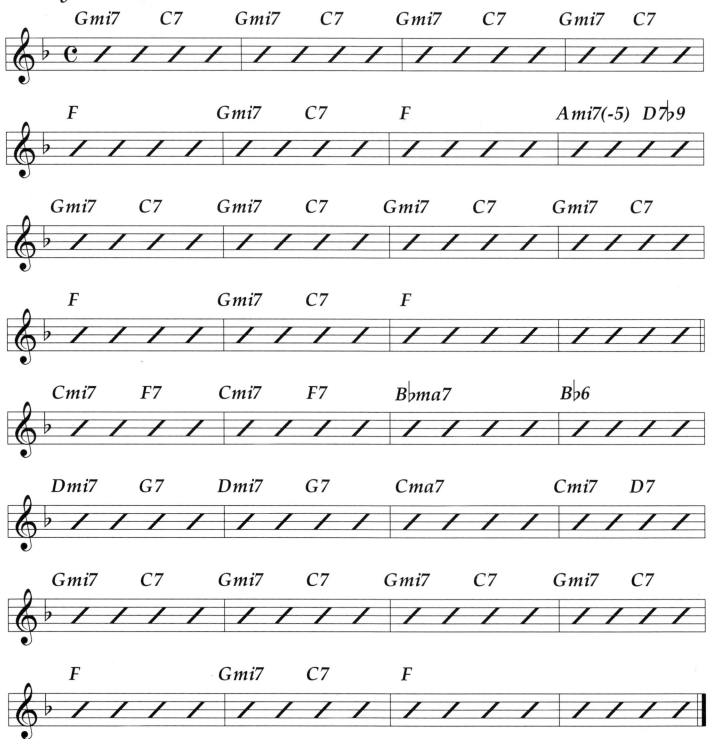

PROGRESSION ANALYSIS

It's difficult to discuss this topic without dealing with aspects of music theory. That would be way beyond the scope of this book, so what I will do instead is give you some shortcuts. You can figure out the theory later.

One thing to remember is not to be overwhelmed by seeing complex chord changes. You can always boil them down to the essentials and come up with a few basic scales that will get you through the tune. For example, when you see any II-V-I progression (like Gmi7-C7-F), you can use the F Major scale to improvise over everything. The same goes for longer progressions. Look at the turnarounds I showed you earlier. See how they are based on ONE scale throughout (except the last one)? Sometimes you do need to use ALL the scales!

My point is that you can figure it out and play it, no matter how hard or complex it may look on the surface. Go back and review all the earlier material. Learn it in ALL keys. Notice how certain things repeat themselves. Basically, dig for yourself. It may sound merciless of me to take you this far and dump you off here, but I think if you have made it to this point in the book and still understand what's going on, you can figure out a lot of it on your own. Frankly, that's how the greats did it. They didn't even have any jazz books.

Here's another shortcut. Know how all modes are based on some scale or another? Well, look at a set of involved changes. What modes or scales go with each chord? NOW, figure out what major or minor scale forms the basis of each mode in the progression. I bet you'll find things suddenly becoming simpler. In fact, try to figure out the three major scales that will allow you to solo over the ENTIRE "Honeysuckle Rose" progression! That is a skill that will get you through almost any chords you will have to solo over.

WHAT NOW?

Okay, you've come this far, your playing has no doubt improved a great deal. You have all these tools at your disposal that you didn't even know about earlier. Now, you're probably asking, "What do I do with them? How do I play something that doesn't sound like babble?"

Well, those are good questions to ask at this point. You are thinking about how to make an original musical statement with your solo. You're at the same point a novelist is when he or she asks themselves what to do with the typewriter sitting in front of them. Well, here are some things to keep in mind:

1) **Tell a story.** That's right. Talk to your audience through your solo. Tell them who you are. Don't always come in blazing with a million notes. Would you interrupt someone's conversation by screaming? That would be rude. Remember, a jazz solo is like a monologue. Franz Josef Haydn, the great Classical composer and teacher of Mozart, referred to his string quartets as "conversations between four intelligent men." Apply that comparison to your soloing. Make your introduction, tell your story, set up your ending, and then hit them with the big punchline. It works every time.

2) **Practice with your brain, but play with your heart.** When you learn the scales and patterns, it should be a very technical process. What you are doing is impressing certain muscle movements into your instinctive memory. You're trying to get them to the point where you don't have to think about them in order to play them correctly. When you're playing a solo, however, it should be a very intuitive, emotional experience. However you feel at that moment, if you're happy, relaxed, sad, angry, sarcastic, if you feel like laughing; whatever it is, *use it*. Channel your feelings through your playing. Make the audience feel it too. If you've practiced correctly, the notes you choose will come out right and your solo will have passion and emotional impact.

3) Listen to all kinds of music. You have to learn certain traditions and conventions of music beyond the scales. If you want to play a certain style (bebop, for example), then listen to the masters of that style. How do they phrase and shape their solos? Are they agitated or laid back? What does it make you feel? Do they use a lot of notes or just a few?

The point is, you have really just started. Don't ever think you have arrived. No matter how good you think you are, there's always someone out there, young and hungry, who can whip your pants. We're all students at this. That's the greatest thing about music. You can keep learning and improving until the day they carry you out the door.

I only hope this book has helped you in your search for improvement. Maybe we will meet one day, play some guitar and you can show me a few things. I'm always looking for new tricks! Until then, keep practicing and GOOD LUCK.

RECOMMENDED LISTENING LIST

These are some of the leading jazz soloists on their instrument. The names are roughly in chronological order. You should be familiar with as many of these musicians as possible, absorbing their styles and mannerisms. My apologies to all the other great players I left off. There just isn't room for everybody!

GUITAR

Django Reinhardt
Charlie Christian
Barney Kessel
Tal Farlow
Jimmy Raney
Wes Montgomery
Jim Hall
Joe Pass
Herb Ellis
George Benson
John McLaughlin
Pat Metheny
John Scofield
Mike Stern

SAXOPHONE

Coleman Hawkins
Lester Young
Charlie Parker
Ben Webster
Hank Mobley
Sonny Stitt
Dexter Gordon
Sonny Rollins
Stan Getz
Pepper Adams
John Coltrane
Ira Sullivan
Joe Henderson
Wayne Shorter
Michael Brecker
Branford Marsalis

CLARINET	Benny Goodman
	Pete Fountain
	Buddy DeFranco
	Eddie Daniels
FLUTE	James Moody
	Yusef Lateef
	Herbie Mann
	Hubert Laws
TRUMPET	Louis Armstrong
	Roy Eldridge
	Dizzy Gillespie
	Fats Navarro
	Miles Davis
	Clifford Brown
	Freddie Hubbard
	Woody Shaw
	Ira Sullivan
	Jon Faddis
	Randy Brecker
	Wynton Marsalis
TROMBONE	Bill Harris
	Kai Winding
	J.J. Johnson
	Bill Watrus
PIANO	Art Tatum
	Bud Powell
	Thelonius Monk
	Red Garland
	Erroll Garner
	Winton Kelly
	Bill Evans
	McCoy Tyner
	Oscar Peterson
	Herbie Hancock
	Chick Corea
	Lyle Mays
	Eliane Elias
	Kenny Kirkland

There are many more, on many other instruments. Hopefully, this list will get you started on a lifetime of listening to (and learning from) great music.

CHORD/SCALE USAGE CHART

This is a simplified chart of the scales most often used to solo over the following families of chords.

Chord Family	Scale Type
Major	Major, Lydian, Bebop Major, Major Pent/Blues
Minor	Minor, Dorian, Minor Pent/Blues
Dominant	Mixolydian, Bebop Dominant, Altered Dominant
Diminished (inc. Dim.7)	Diminished
Augmented (inc. Aug.7)	Wholetone, Altered Dominant
Altered	Altered Dominant, Wholetone, Lydian b7
Half Diminished (Min7^{b5})	Locrian, Super

NOTES

NOTES